QUICK MAIN DISHES

Delicious family meals in 30 minutes or less

CONTENTS

Guide to symbols

The recipes in this book are accompanied by symbols that alert you to important information.

 Tells you how many people the recipe serves, or how much is produced.

 Indicates how much time you will need to prepare and cook a dish. Next to this symbol you will also find out if additional time is required for such things as marinating, standing, proving, or cooling. You need to read the recipe to find out exactly how much extra time is needed.

 Alerts you to what has to be done before you can begin to cook the recipe, or to parts of the recipe that take a long time to complete.

 Denotes that special equipment is required. Where possible, alternatives are given.

 Accompanies freezing information.

Herb and goat's cheese frittata

Thinner than a Spanish tortilla, this Italian dish is ideal for light meals.

INGREDIENTS

6 eggs
4 sage leaves, finely chopped
salt and freshly ground black pepper
3 tbsp olive oil, plus extra
   for brushing
1 shallot, chopped
10 cherry tomatoes, halved
115g (4oz) goat's cheese, rind
   removed if necessary, and crumbled

METHOD

1 Preheat the grill on its highest setting and position the rack 10cm (4in) from the heat. Beat the eggs in a bowl with the sage, season to taste with salt and pepper, and set aside.

2 Heat the oil in the frying pan over a medium heat. Add the shallot and fry, stirring constantly, for 3 minutes, or until just softened but not browned.

3 Add the eggs to the pan and stir gently to combine. Reduce the heat, then cover and leave to cook gently for 10–15 minutes before removing the lid; the frittata should still be runny on top.

4 Arrange the tomatoes and goat's cheese over the surface and lightly brush with olive oil. Transfer the pan to the grill for 5 minutes or until the frittata is set and lightly browned. Leave to stand for 5 minutes before cutting into wedges. Serve warm or cooled.

serves 4

prep 10 mins
• cook 20 mins

23cm (9in) non-stick
frying pan with a lid
and flameproof handle

Cauliflower cheese

A great comfort food side dish that works equally well as a vegetarian main course.

INGREDIENTS
1 head of cauliflower, outer leaves removed,
    separated into large florets
salt and freshly ground black pepper
100g (3½oz) fresh breadcrumbs

For the cheese sauce
30g (1oz) butter, diced
3 tbsp plain white or
    wholemeal flour
1½ tsp mustard powder
450ml (15fl oz) milk
125g (4½oz) mature Cheddar cheese, grated

METHOD
1 Bring a large saucepan of salted water to the boil. Add the cauliflower florets and boil for 7 minutes, or until just tender. Drain well and rinse with cold water to stop the cooking. Arrange the florets in an ovenproof serving dish.

2 Preheat the grill on its highest setting. To make the cheese sauce, melt the butter in a pan over a low heat, add the flour and mustard powder, and stir to combine. Cook for 2 minutes, stirring all the time. Remove from the heat, add the milk, and stir constantly until smooth. Return to the heat and bring slowly to the boil, then reduce the heat and simmer to thicken for 1–2 minutes. Remove the pan from the heat and stir in three-quarters of the cheese until melted. Season to taste with salt and pepper, then pour the sauce over the florets.

3 Toss the remaining cheese with the breadcrumbs and sprinkle over the florets. Place the dish under the grill for 10 minutes, or until the sauce bubbles and the top is golden. Serve hot from the dish.

serves 4-6

prep 15 mins
• cook 15 mins

Vegetable kebabs

Cook these under the grill or on a barbecue.

INGREDIENTS
1 courgette
1 red pepper, deseeded
1 green pepper, deseeded
1 red onion
8 cherry tomatoes
8 button mushrooms
5 tbsp olive oil
1 garlic clove, crushed
½ tsp dried oregano
pinch of chilli flakes

METHOD
1 Trim the courgette and cut into 8 chunks. Cut the peppers into 2.5cm (1in) pieces.
  Peel the onion, and cut into wedges, leaving the root end intact so that the wedges do
  not fall apart.
2 Thread the vegetables on to 4 large or 8 small skewers. Whisk the remaining ingredients
  together in a small bowl with a fork to make a flavoured oil.
3 Preheat the grill on a medium-high setting. Place the kebabs on the grill rack and brush
  generously with the flavoured oil. Cook for 10–15 minutes, or until the vegetables are just
  tender, turning frequently and brushing with more of the oil as you do so. Drizzle any
  remaining oil over the cooked kebabs.

 serves 4

 prep 15 mins
• cook 15 mins

 wooden
skewers

 soak wooden skewers
in cold water for 30
mins before using, to
prevent burning

Chilli tofu stir-fry

This quick and easy dish plays on tofu's ability to take on the flavour of other ingredients.

INGREDIENTS

2 tbsp sunflower oil
85g (3oz) unsalted cashew nuts
300g (10oz) firm tofu, cubed
1 red onion, thinly sliced
2 carrots, peeled and thinly sliced
1 red pepper, deseeded and chopped
1 celery stick, chopped
4 chestnut mushrooms, sliced
175g (6oz) beansprouts
2 tsp chilli sauce
2 tbsp light soy sauce
1 tsp cornflour
175ml (6fl oz) vegetable stock

METHOD

1 Heat the oil in a wok and add the cashews; stir-fry for 30 seconds, or until lightly browned. Drain and set aside.

2 Add the tofu and stir-fry until golden. Drain and set aside. Stir-fry the onion and carrots for 5 minutes, then add the red pepper, celery, and mushrooms and stir-fry for 3–4 minutes. Finally, add the beansprouts and stir-fry for 2 minutes. Keep the heat under the wok high, so the vegetables fry quickly.

3 Return the cashews and tofu to the pan and drizzle in the chilli sauce. In a small bowl, mix the soy sauce with the cornflour and pour into the pan, along with the stock. Toss over the heat for 2–3 minutes, or until the sauce is bubbling. Serve with rice or noodles.

serves 4

prep 10 mins
• cook 15 mins

wok

Tomato bulgur wheat with capers and olives

This dish gives Middle-Eastern bulgur wheat a Mediterranean character.

INGREDIENTS

350g (12oz) bulgur wheat
salt and freshly ground black pepper
150–300ml (5–10fl oz) tomato juice
3 tsp capers in vinegar, drained
12 black olives, pitted and halved
12 green olives, pitted and halved

METHOD

1 Tip the bulgur wheat into a large bowl, then pour over enough boiling water just to cover – about 300ml (10fl oz). Leave to stand for about 15 minutes.
2 Season generously with salt and black pepper, and stir well with a fork to fluff up the grains. Add the tomato juice, a little at a time, until the bulgur has absorbed all the juice. Leave to stand for a few minutes between each addition – the bulgur will absorb quite a lot of moisture.
3 Now add the capers and olives, taste, and season again if needed. Serve with a crisp green salad and some warm pitta bread.

serves 4

**prep 15 mins
plus standing
• cook 15 mins**

Olive and anchovy open tart

Storecupboard ingredients make this a perfect dish when time is short.

INGREDIENTS

375g (13oz) ready-made puff pastry
1 egg, lightly beaten, for egg wash
3 tbsp tomato passata
12 unsalted anchovies in oil, drained
12 black olives, pitted
freshly ground black pepper

METHOD

1 Preheat the oven to 200°C (400°F/Gas 6). Roll out the pastry, and lay on a baking tray. Using a sharp knife, score a line about 5cm (2in) in from the edges all the way around to form a border, but do not cut all the way through the pastry. Next, using the back of the knife, score the pastry all the way around the outer edges. This helps it to puff up when cooking.

2 Brush the border with the egg wash, then smooth the passata over the inside area, spreading up to the scored edges. Arrange the anchovies and olives over the tart, and sprinkle over a pinch of black pepper.

3 Bake in the oven for about 15 minutes, until the pastry is cooked and the edges are puffed and golden. Cut into 6 squares, and serve warm with a crisp green salad.

serves 6

prep 15 mins
• cook 15 mins

Tomato and harissa tart

Harissa gives this tart a fiery kick.

INGREDIENTS
400g (14oz) ready-made puff pastry
flour, for dusting
2 tbsp red pepper pesto
6 tomatoes, halved
2–3 tbsp harissa paste
1 tbsp olive oil
few sprigs of thyme, leaves picked

METHOD
1 Preheat the oven to 200°C (400°F/Gas 6). Roll out the pastry on a floured work surface, into a large rectangle or square. Lay on a baking tray, then use a sharp knife to score a border about 5cm (2in) in from the edges all the way around, being careful not to cut all the way through the pastry. Next, using the back of the knife, score the pastry around the outer edges – this will help it to puff up.

2 Working inside the border, smother the pastry with the pesto. Arrange the tomatoes on top, cut side up. Mix the harissa with the olive oil, and drizzle over the tomatoes. Scatter the thyme leaves over.

3 Bake in the oven for about 15 minutes until the pastry is cooked and golden. Serve hot.

serves 6

prep 10 mins
• cook 15 mins

Penne with sausage and artichoke

The robust flavours of this pasta dish will have you coming back for more.

INGREDIENTS

1 tbsp olive oil
1 onion, finely diced
salt and freshly ground black pepper
1 red chilli, deseeded and finely chopped
6 good-quality pork sausages,
  skinned and chopped
pinch of dried oregano
400g jar or can artichoke hearts,
  drained and roughly chopped
3 tomatoes, skinned and diced
handful of pitted black olives
350g (12oz) dried penne

METHOD

1 Heat the oil in a large frying pan, add the onion and a pinch of salt, and cook over a low heat for 5 minutes, or until soft and translucent. Add the chilli and cook for a few seconds more, then add the sausages, breaking them up with the back of a fork until they are roughly mashed. Cook for about 10 minutes, until they are no longer pink, stirring occasionally, then add the oregano and artichokes and cook for a few minutes more. Stir in the tomatoes and olives, then season well with salt and black pepper.

2 Meanwhile, cook the pasta in a large pan of boiling salted water for 10 minutes, or until it is cooked but still firm to the bite. Drain, keeping back a tiny amount of the cooking water. Return the pasta to the pan and toss together. Combine with the sausage mixture and serve.

serves 4

prep 10 mins
• cook 20 mins

Linguine alle vongole

Versions of this popular classic of linguine and clams are cooked all along the Italian Mediterranean and Adriatic coasts.

INGREDIENTS

2 tbsp olive oil
1 onion, finely chopped
2 garlic cloves, finely chopped
400g can chopped tomatoes
2 tbsp sun-dried tomato purée
120ml (4fl oz) dry white wine
2 x 140g jars clams in natural juice,
    strained, with the juice reserved
salt and freshly ground black pepper
350g (12oz) dried linguine
4 tbsp finely chopped flat-leaf parsley,
    plus extra to garnish

METHOD

1 Heat the oil in a large saucepan over medium heat. Add the onion and garlic and fry, stirring frequently, for 5 minutes or until softened. Add the tomatoes with their juices, tomato purée, wine, and reserved clam juice, and season to taste with salt and pepper, then bring to the boil, stirring. Reduce the heat to low, partially cover the pan and leave to simmer for 10–15 minutes, stirring occasionally.

2 Meanwhile, bring a large pan of salted water to the boil over a high heat. Add the linguine, stir and boil for 10 minutes, or until the pasta is tender but firm to the bite. Drain the pasta into a large colander and shake to remove any excess water.

3 Add the clams and chopped parsley to the sauce and continue to simmer for 1–2 minutes to heat through. Season with salt and pepper to taste.

4 Add the linguine to the sauce and use 2 forks to toss and combine all the ingredients so the pasta is well coated and the clams evenly distributed. Sprinkle with extra parsley and serve at once.

serves 4

prep 5 mins
• cook 30 mins

Sweet and sour prawns

Prawns stir-fried in a fragrant sauce flavoured with chilli, garlic, and ginger.

INGREDIENTS

3 tbsp rice wine vinegar

2 tbsp clear honey

1 tbsp caster sugar

2 tbsp light soy sauce

2 tbsp tomato ketchup

2 tbsp vegetable oil

3 shallots, peeled and sliced

2cm (¾in) piece of fresh root
   ginger, peeled and grated

1 red chilli, deseeded and
   finely chopped

1 garlic clove, crushed

1 small carrot, cut into matchsticks

1 celery stick, cut into matchsticks

1 green pepper, deseeded and cut
   into strips

500g (1lb 2oz) raw tiger prawns,
   peeled and deveined

2 spring onions, sliced lengthways,
   to garnish

METHOD

1 Heat the first 5 ingredients together in a small saucepan, until the honey and sugar melt. Remove from the heat and set aside.

2 Heat the oil in a wok, add the shallots, ginger, chilli, garlic, carrot, celery, and green pepper and stir-fry for 4 minutes.

3 Add the prawns and stir-fry for a further 2 minutes or until the prawns turn pink. Pour in the vinegar-and-sugar mixture and stir-fry for 1 minute, or until the prawns and vegetables are coated and everything is heated through.

4 To serve, transfer to a platter and garnish with spring onions. Serve with boiled rice.

serves 4

prep 20 mins
• cook 10 mins

wok

Salad Niçoise

This famous French classic is substantial enough to be served as a main dish.

INGREDIENTS

150g (5½oz) green beans, trimmed
4 x 150g (5½oz) tuna steaks
extra virgin olive oil, for brushing
8 anchovy fillets in olive oil, drained
1 red onion, finely sliced
250g (9oz) plum tomatoes,
   quartered lengthways
12 black olives
2 romaine lettuce hearts, trimmed
   and torn into bite-sized pieces
8–10 basil leaves
4 eggs, hard–boiled

For the vinaigrette

2 tsp Dijon mustard
1 garlic clove, finely chopped
3 tbsp white wine vinegar
150ml (5fl oz) extra virgin olive oil,
juice of ½ lemon
salt and freshly ground black pepper

METHOD

1 Cook the green beans in a saucepan of gently boiling water, for 3–4 minutes, or until just tender. Drain the beans and quickly place them into a bowl of ice water.
2 Preheat a ridged grill pan over a medium-high heat. Brush the tuna steaks with 1–2 tablespoons of olive oil and season to taste with salt and pepper. Sear the tuna steaks for 2 minutes on each side. The centres will still be slightly pink. Set the tuna aside. Drain the green beans.
3 Meanwhile, to make the vinaigrette, whisk together the Dijon mustard, garlic, vinegar, olive oil, and lemon juice. Season to taste with salt and pepper.
4 Place the green beans, anchovies, onion, tomatoes, olives, lettuce, and basil in a large bowl. Drizzle with the vinaigrette and gently toss.
5 Divide the salad between 4 plates. Peel and quarter each egg and add them to the plates. Cut each tuna steak in half and arrange both halves on top of the salad.

serves 4

prep 25 mins
• cook 10 mins

ridged grill pan

Baked plaice with bacon

This is a tasty and unusual way of cooking flat fish.

INGREDIENTS

2 tbsp olive oil
4 back bacon rashers, chopped
3 spring onions, chopped
4 plaice fillets, 175g (6oz) each
freshly ground black pepper
60g (2oz) butter
juice of ½ large lemon
1 tbsp chopped parsley

METHOD

1 Preheat the oven to 200°C (400°F/Gas 6). Heat the oil in a roasting tin over medium heat, add the bacon and spring onions, and fry for 2 minutes, stirring frequently.
2 Add the plaice, skin-side down, baste with the oil, and season to taste with pepper.
3 Place the tin in the oven and bake the fish for 15 minutes, basting once or twice.
4 Transfer the cooked plaice to warmed serving plates. Drain the bacon and spring onions from the tin and set aside.
5 Heat the butter in a small saucepan until golden brown, add the lemon juice, bacon, and onions, and stir in the parsley. Spoon over the plaice and serve at once with steamed vegetables, such as spinach, green beans, or carrots.

serves 4

prep 10 mins
• cook 20 mins

Chinese-style steamed bass

This impressive restaurant-style dish is surprisingly easy to prepare.

INGREDIENTS

8 tbsp soy sauce

8 tbsp Chinese rice wine or dry sherry

6 tbsp thinly sliced fresh root ginger

4 small sea bass, gutted and rinsed

2 tbsp sesame oil

1 tsp salt

4 spring onions, trimmed and thinly sliced

8 tbsp sunflower oil

4 garlic cloves, chopped

2 small red chillies, deseeded and thinly sliced

thinly sliced zest of 2 limes

METHOD

1 Prepare a steamer, or position a steaming rack in a wok with water so it doesn't touch the water. Bring to the boil.

2 Stir together the soy sauce, rice wine, and 4 tbsp ginger, and set aside. Using a sharp knife, make slashes in the fish, 2.5cm (1in) apart and not quite as deep as the bone, on both sides. Rub the fish inside and out with the sesame oil and salt.

3 Scatter one-quarter of the spring onions over a heatproof serving dish that will hold 2 fish and fit in the steamer or on the steaming rack. Place 2 fish on the dish and pour over half the sauce.

4 Place the dish in the steamer or on the rack, cover, and steam for 10–12 minutes, or until the fish is cooked through and flakes easily when tested with a knife. Remove the fish, cover, and keep warm. Repeat with the remaining fish.

5 Meanwhile, heat the sunflower oil in a small saucepan over a medium-high heat until shimmering. Scatter the fish with remaining spring onions and ginger, and the garlic, chilli, and lime zest. Drizzle the hot oil over the fish and serve.

serves 4

prep 15 mins
• cook 10-12 mins

steamer, or a wok
with steaming
rack and lid

Seared tuna with cucumber and fennel

This tuna is served very rare, so use the freshest possible fish.

INGREDIENTS

6 tbsp olive oil, plus extra for brushing
4 x 150g (5½oz) tuna steaks
salt and freshly ground black pepper
1 fennel bulb, sliced
2 shallots, finely chopped
1 cucumber, deseeded, skinned and finely chopped

30g (1oz) mint, parsley and chervil leaves, torn and mixed
juice of 1 lemon
8 anchovy fillets
lemon wedges, to serve

METHOD

1 Rub 2 tablespoons of oil over the tuna steaks and sprinkle with lots of black pepper. Set aside.
2 Heat 2 tablespoons of olive oil and sauté the fennel for 4–5 minutes, or until just tender. Season with salt and pepper. Tip the fennel into a large bowl and set aside to cool a little.
3 Add the shallots, cucumber, and herbs to the fennel. Stir in the lemon juice and remaining oil.
4 Heat a heavy frying pan or grill pan until smoking. Lightly brush the tuna steaks with oil, then pan-fry for 30 seconds. Brush the top with a little more oil, turn over, and cook for a further 30 seconds.
5 Place a tuna steak on each serving plate, with the salad piled on top, and 2 anchovies draped over. Drizzle with the remaining lemon and oil from the bowl, and serve with a wedge of lemon. This dish is good with a salad of warm parsley-buttered new potatoes.

serves 4

prep 15 mins
plus cooling
• cook 6 mins

Thai green chicken curry

This flavoursome dish can be made speedily using a jar of Thai curry paste.

INGREDIENTS

1 tbsp olive oil
4 tsp Thai green curry paste (use
  more paste for a spicier sauce)
4 skinless boneless chicken breasts,
  about 140g (5oz) each, cut into
  bite-sized pieces
2 tbsp light soy sauce
400ml can coconut milk
175g (6oz) open-cap
  mushrooms, chopped
6 spring onions, trimmed, with the green
  part cut into 5mm (¼in) slices
salt and freshly ground black pepper
chopped coriander, to garnish

METHOD

1 Heat the oil in a large frying pan over a medium heat. Add the curry paste and stir.
  Add the chicken and stir-fry for 2 minutes, or until lightly browned.
2 Pour in the soy sauce and coconut milk and bring to the boil, stirring. Lower the
  heat, stir in the mushrooms and most of the spring onions, and season with salt
  and pepper to taste, then simmer for about 8 minutes, or until the chicken is tender
  and cooked through.
3 Garnish with coriander and the remaining sliced spring onions, and serve hot with
  boiled rice.

serves 4

**prep 10 mins
• cook 10 mins**

Chicken and noodle stir-fry

A colourful Chinese favourite, packed with contrasting flavours and textures.

INGREDIENTS

1 tbsp vegetable oil

2 skinless boneless chicken breasts, cut into bite-sized pieces

½ red pepper, deseeded and chopped

½ green pepper, deseeded and chopped

½ yellow pepper or orange pepper, deseeded and chopped

2.5cm (1in) piece of fresh root ginger, peeled and grated

115g (4oz) shiitake mushrooms, quartered

120ml (4fl oz) chicken stock

2 tbsp tomato ketchup

2 tbsp light soy sauce

1 tsp cornflour

350g (12oz) fresh medium egg noodles

toasted sesame oil, for drizzling

2 tbsp sesame seeds, for garnish

METHOD

1 Heat the vegetable oil in a wok until hot. Add the chicken and stir-fry for 3 minutes. Remove and set aside.

2 Add the peppers, ginger, and mushrooms to the wok and stir-fry for 3 minutes.

3 Mix together the chicken stock, ketchup, soy sauce, and cornflour until smooth. Return the chicken to the wok, add the noodles, and pour in the stock mixture. Toss everything together over the heat for 3 minutes, or until piping hot.

4 Just before serving, drizzle with sesame oil, sprinkle the sesame seeds on top, and serve.

 serves 4

 prep 20 mins • cook 10 mins

 wok

Devilled turkey

Serve these spicy stir-fried turkey strips as a healthy lunch or supper.

INGREDIENTS

2 tbsp wholegrain mustard

2 tbsp mango chutney

2 tbsp Worcestershire sauce

¼ tsp ground paprika

3 tbsp orange juice

1 red chilli, chopped (optional)

2 tbsp olive oil

450g (1lb) turkey breast escalope,
    cut into strips

1 onion, peeled and finely chopped

1 red pepper, cored and cut into strips

1 orange pepper, cored and cut
    into strips

1 garlic clove, crushed

METHOD

1 Mix the mustard, chutney, Worcestershire sauce, paprika, orange juice, and chilli (if using) together until well combined.

2 Heat the oil in a frying pan or wok, add the turkey, and cook over a high heat until browned. Remove the turkey from the pan and set aside, covered to keep it warm.

3 Add the onion to the pan and fry for 2–3 minutes, or until beginning to colour. Add the peppers and garlic and fry, stirring constantly, for 3–4 minutes, or until tender.

4 Stir in the mustard mixture and return the turkey to the pan. Cook for 5 minutes, stirring, or until piping hot and the turkey is cooked through.

makes 12

prep 10 mins
• cook 15 mins

Beef tacos

A convenient family supper dish, tacos are filling and require no cutlery.

INGREDIENTS

1 tbsp olive oil
1 onion, finely chopped
salt
2 garlic cloves, grated or
    finely chopped
1 fresh green chilli, deseeded
    and finely chopped
675g (1½lb) lean beef mince
300ml (10fl oz) hot vegetable stock
4 tomatoes, skinned and chopped
handful of fresh coriander,
    finely chopped
8 taco shells
75g (2½oz) strong Cheddar
    cheese, grated

METHOD

1 Preheat the grill to hot. Heat the oil in a frying pan over a medium heat. Add the onion and a pinch of salt, and sauté for a couple of minutes until soft and translucent. Add the garlic and chilli, and sauté for a few seconds before adding the beef mince. Cook, stirring, until no longer pink, adding just enough of the stock to prevent the meat sticking, but not so much that it gets too wet.

2 When the beef is cooked, stir in the tomatoes and coriander. Spoon the mixture into the tacos, and top each one with grated cheese. Sit the tacos upright in an ovenproof dish, and put under the grill until the cheese has melted. Serve hot.

serves 4

prep 15 mins
• cook 15 mins

Hamburgers

Burgers are classic American fare.

INGREDIENTS

450g (1lb) lean minced steak
½ onion, very finely chopped
1 egg yolk
salt and freshly ground black pepper
olive oil or sunflower oil
4 sesame seed baps, cut in half and
  lightly toasted

METHOD

1 Place the minced beef and chopped onions in a mixing bowl, add the egg yolk, season
  to taste with salt and pepper, and mix well.
2 Divide the mixture into 4 equal portions and, using wet hands, shape them into
  4 burgers.
3 Preheat a griddle pan or grill on its highest setting. Lightly oil the griddle pan and grill
  the burgers for 3 minutes on each side, or longer if you prefer.
4 Serve in toasted sesame buns with your favourite toppings, such as sliced onions, sliced
  tomatoes, lettuce, pickles, tomato ketchup, mayonnaise, and mustard.

serves 4

prep 15 mins
• cook 10 mins

freeze the uncooked
hamburgers for
up to 3 months

Pork chops with green peppercorn sauce

These soft, mild peppercorns add a gentle spice to the creamy sauce.

INGREDIENTS

4 lean pork loin chops
salt and freshly ground black pepper
1 tbsp sunflower oil
30g (1oz) butter
1 large shallot, finely chopped
4 tbsp dry sherry
1½ tbsp green peppercorns in brine,
   rinsed,
   drained and lightly crushed
150ml (5fl oz) chicken stock
4 tbsp crème fraîche

METHOD

1 Trim the chops of excess fat and season with salt and pepper. Heat the oil in a large, heavy frying pan on medium heat and fry the chops for 6–8 minutes on each side, depending on thickness, until golden brown and the juices run clear. Remove from the pan to a warm plate and cover with foil.

2 To make the sauce, melt the butter in the pan and fry the shallot over medium heat for 4–5 minutes, stirring often, until soft but not browned. Stir in the sherry and simmer for about 1 minute. Add the peppercorns and stock, bring to the boil and simmer for 2–3 minutes, or until slightly reduced.

3 Stir in the crème fraîche, spoon the sauce over the chops and serve immediately. Try this paired with potato rösti cakes and steamed green vegetables.

makes 12   prep 10 mins
                  • cook 15 mins

Sauté of liver, bacon, and onions

Tender calf's liver is the perfect partner to salty bacon and a rich sauce.

INGREDIENTS

350g (12oz) calf's liver
200g (7oz) sweet-cured, smoked streaky
  bacon thin-cut rashers
1 tbsp olive oil
25g (scant 1oz) unsalted butter
4 shallots, thinly sliced

120ml (4fl oz) vermouth
1 tsp Dijon mustard
dash of mushroom ketchup or
  Worcestershire sauce (optional)
salt and freshly ground black pepper

METHOD

1 Cut the liver and the bacon rashers into strips about 6cm (2¼in) long and
  1.5cm (½in) wide. Set aside.

2 Heat half the oil and half the butter in a frying pan over a medium heat, add the
  shallots, and fry, stirring frequently, for 5 minutes, or until soft and golden. Remove
  from the pan and reserve.

3 Add the remaining oil and butter to the pan and increase the heat to high. Add the
  liver and bacon and stir-fry for 3–4 minutes, until the liver is cooked but still slightly
  pink inside.

4 Return the shallots to the pan, pour in the vermouth, and let it bubble for 1–2 minutes,
  scraping any bits stuck to the bottom of the pan.

5 Reduce the heat to medium and stir in the mustard and the mushroom ketchup (if using).
  Serve at once with creamy mashed potato and green beans.

serves 4

prep 10 mins
• cook 10 mins

Thai-style minced pork with noodles

Low in fat, this tasty and speedy stir-fry is perfect for a light meal.

INGREDIENTS

1 tbsp vegetable oil

675g (1½lb) pork mince

4 garlic cloves, grated or finely
  chopped

salt

2 fresh red chillies, deseeded
  and finely chopped

juice of 1 lime

1 tbsp Thai fish sauce, such as
  nam pla

1 tbsp dark soy sauce

handful of fresh coriander,
  finely chopped

medium rice noodles or rice,
  to server

METHOD

1 Heat the oil in a wok or large frying pan over a medium-high heat. Add the pork, garlic, and a pinch of salt. Stir-fry until no longer pink, tossing continuously.

2 Add the chillies, lime juice, fish sauce, and soy sauce, and stir-fry for a further 5 minutes.

3 When ready to serve, sprinkle over the coriander, and stir well. Serve hot with noodles or rice.

serves 4

prep 10 mins
• cook 15 mins

Senior Editor   Cécile Landau

Designer   Elma Aquino

Jacket Designer   Mark Penfound

Special Sales Creative Project Manager   Alison Donovan

Pre-Production Producer   Rob Dunn

Producer   Igrain Roberts

DK INDIA

Editorial Consultant   Dipali Singh

Designer   Neha Ahuja

DTP Designer   Tarun Sharma

DTP Coordinator   Sunil Sharma

Head of Publishing   Aparna Sharma

This paperback edition published in 2017
First published in Great Britain in 2013
Material previously published in
The Cooking Book (2008) and *Cook Express* (2009)
by Dorling Kindersley Limited , 80 Strand, London WC2R 0RL

Copyright © 2008, 2009, 2013, 2017 Dorling Kindersley

2 4 6 8 10 9 7 5 3 1
001–192534–Nov/2017

A CIP catalogue record for this book is available from the British Library.

ISBN 978-0-2413-1821-8

Printed and bound in China

A WORLD OF IDEAS
SEE ALL THERE IS TO KNOW

www.dk.com